Lie In Silence

Hailey Royse

BookLeaf Publishing

India | USA | UK

Made with ❤ on the BookLeaf Publishing Platform
www.bookleafpub.in
www.bookleafpub.com

Dedication

To anyone who has felt overwhelmed by the weight of life.

Preface

The path may seem lonely, but know you are not
alone.
I hope each poem will reassure you.
You are seen, you are heard, you are understood.
May this book be a gentle reminder
that the darkest moments are only a single moment in a
long life.

Acknowledgements

1. Moth To A Flame

A spark leads to a flame
a flame radiant like a sunrise
golden rays sting your eyes
a promised glimpse of beauty
has you stare until your blind

A flame fills your nose
with a sickly sweet smoke
lingering behind each closed door
every deep breath
has you aching for more

A flame envelops you in its warmth
waves pull you in
till you touch a blistering heat
leaving burns that
bring you to your knees

A flame could never taste as bittersweet
though flushed lips savor honey
bitter lies on your tongue
burning each taste bud
so nothing will taste the same again

A flame does not start with a roar
it snaps here and there
snaps turn into explosions
filling rooms with echos, so loud
you can't help but listen

A flame blinds you,
fills your every breath
a flame with a blistering touch,
burns each taste bud
a flame meant to sound like peace,
sounded a raging war

I willingly surrendered all senses
to be senseless with a flame

2. Good Morning

If I lie in wait
for the heavens to scorch my skin
how long do I lay
for the demons within

Is it born of hate
this darkness that wishes to win
can I survive a world of grey
with my strength growing thin

Will the light change my fate
help me forget each sin
waiting for the warmth of each ray
till I open my eyes again.

3. Seven Years Of Silence

I was led blind
By a voice that gave me no peace of mind
A new beginning in the dead of night
A change I tried to fight

A single word, now a walking contradiction
Gloom towers over me, with unwelcome friction
Once still waters, now scourge as I lay
I never knew my body could betray

4 (Haiku). After Dark

5

Wars waging within
Each bullet grazing my skin
Demons want to win

5. Muted

A voice taut
listen, don't speak

.

A voice left
rights to be wronged.

Lost to the current
battle waging

A voice barely present
wrapped in worry

A voice rose
thorns tore it apart

Will I hurt myself more?
Or can I break this silence?

6. Bleeding Heart

I sit in silence
unspoken words in each breath
heart and soul left shattered

all I do is stare at the floor
where I bled my heart dry
for you

every drop spilled on the stretched cloth
without a second glance
from you

my heart and soul weren't enough
when has it ever been
with you?

in the silence
I hold a smile long enough to hide
beside you.

7 (Haiku). Poisonous

Words with a strong bite
Venom that burns in my eyes
I hide a choked cry

8. Twisted Fairytales

When we are young
villains are drawn for you to fear
crooked smiles, reptilian skin
scars on tattered souls

No one drew villains with
sparkling smiles, unblemished skin
strong physiques
how were you supposed to know?

Villains don't sit in the shadows
they don't hide in dark forests or
dense fog in the dead of night

Real villains blind you
with the shimmer of a castle
gentle hands that guide you to light
before shattering the illusion

Perfectly drawn fantasies
promised a prince
to save you from all the villains

But every prince
has turned out to be a villain
drawn by reality

9 . The sun

A glowing beauty pulls all into her orbit

golden rays fall past her shoulder
making every star dim
reaching for warmth
to be burned when you get too close
she blinds all
she is blind to all

She is the sun

10. The Moon

A beauty only allowed to glow in the dark

she can not blind the sky with light
but rages wars of water at will
she embraces all
lets every star shine
to be forgotten with the sunrise
she drifts away more each day

She is the moon

11 (Haiku). Aspirations

Each laugh had me break
Hopes shattered with every sound
You couldn't be proud?

12 (Haiku). Choices

If I speak my mind
Your rage brings me to my knees
Instead, I'm silent

13. Inner Cheerleader

In the quiet
the noise grows loud

a noise I cannot see
a noise I cannot fight
it fills every sense
hides behind my eyes
ringing in my ears

always the same chant
YOU. ARE. NOT. ENOUGH.

14. Empty Voice

My mouth, sewn shut
by a thread of worry
a thread no one can see

liking how I listen
with a tear-soaked shoulder
blind to the fact I don't speak

pulling at the seams
is an endless struggle
always draining me

looking past the pain in my eyes
to express what's in your heart
is slowly killing me

feelings eat away at me
begging to be let out
begging to speak

I wish for scissors
to cut each thread
so you'd listen to me

15. A Bluebird and Elk

The Bird soars, reaching unseen heights
she travels from first-light
until deep into the night
if winds were more steady
she'd make it to her nest
before the sun lies on land

The Elk with towering horns
to protect from harm
roamed vast lands
Scared to call any home
a generous forest
only reminds him he's alone

The Elk called to the skies above
as the Bird looked down below
one saw beauty in shades of blue
another saw stability, in horns held tall
too different worlds
having to rise and fall

A strange wind blew, shaking mountains
they built common ground on
the bird sang a song about her day above

but the Elk always questioned
he had never heard a song like his blue bird's
wanting to know every key and note

The Elk traveled rocky terrain
lead by a steady mind
but the Bird flies with the wind
letting it guide her to new heights

Are they simply from too different worlds?
Or is it simple?
Put in the work.

16. Thicker then water

"We are family"
Thud...

"Don't you care?"
Thud, Thud...

"In the end, we are all you have."
Thud, Thud, Thud...

My heart never knows peace.

17. Anxiety

I dive in the water
with a current too strong
it pulls me under

again and again
I kick and kick

trying to break the surface
the pressure builds in my lungs

the more I yell out
the more water I let in

the more I try
the more I tire
Instead, I try to stay afloat

18 (Haiku).

NOTIFICATION

life, frozen in pain
living in a memory
till three years have passed

19. Conditional Love

I beg for your love / I search for your praise / I wish for your kindness / After all my longing / I'm thrown into a jarring reality / Love is never given freely

20 (Sestina). In madness lies sanity

No one is told how to live life
many become lost in the past
some strive to stay in the present
others worry about the future
everyone trying to keep sane
never show their madness

Each memory creates madness
shaping my choices in life
running in circles like I'm insane
each memory feeling less like the past
has me questioning my future
wishing I was present

Envious of those who live in the present
not driven to madness
by the unknown future
of their life
envious of those not haunted by their past
without trauma, I'd be sane

Is it sane
to not to be present
choosing to hold on to the past
no, it must be madness
craving a love lost to life
praying for it again in the future

I can't hold on to the future
I dreamt; it's insane
I can't live a life
where you're not present
many call it madness
but at least I have you in my past

My happiness lives in our past
one I can not mirror in the future
tired of this madness
wishing to be sane
I have to face the present
in hopes of moving on with life